Luxemburg, Rosa

Letters from prison

Inktank publishing

Luxemburg, Rosa

Letters from prison

Inktank publishing, 2018

www.inktank-publishing.com

ISBN/EAN: 9783747776360

ROSA LUXEMBURG

LETTERS FROM PRISON

WITH A PORTRAIT AND A FACSIMILE

Translated from the German
by
Eden & Cedar Paul

1923

PUBLISHING HOUSE OF THE YOUNG INTERNATIONAL
BERLIN-SCHOENEBERG / FEURIGSTR. 63

PRINTED IN GERMANY

PREFACTORY REMARK

DURING the war Rosa Luxemburg spent three years and four months in prison. One year — from February 1915 to February 1916 — in a prison in Berlin (Barnimstrasse) for a speech she made in Frankfurt-on-the-Main against military abuses, and another two years and four months — from July 1916 to November 10th, 1918 — in "preventive detention" in Berlin, Wronke and Breslau. She was entirely cut off from the outside world, and was allowed to receive only such books and letters as had passed a rigid censorship. Once a month she was allowed to receive visitors, but only under strict supervision.

This punishment was intended to crush the willpower of this most courageous protagonist of the proletariat, and to silence that voice of hers that was ever calling to action, ever branding lies and ever proclaiming the truth. Both these intentions failed. Her iron willpower was not lamed. Throughout her whole term of imprisonment Rosa Luxemburg worked on untiringly. The indescribable loneliness of endless days and nights brought out all the powers of her intellect and spirit. Her passion for knowledge broke forth in fanfare tones: the famous *Junius Pamphlet* written behind prison bars was not the only summons to action that found its way out of the prison gates. Hand-bills, appeals, and important supplements to the *Spartacus Letters* were transmitted to the friends of Rosa Luxemburg. By means of keen, stinging illegal correspondence and by means of other activities she tried, even in her cell, to guide the revolutionary development of the German working class.

But we do not intend at this juncture to write an appreciation of her scientific and her agitating activities during these terrible years. All we wish to do is to show to the young and to the older workers, to all those for whose welfare and liberty she fought, suffered and died — done to death by cowardly criminal hands — the true character of this greatly maligned woman. And in her case there can be no longer any reason for withholding these letters from publication. These letters have ceased to be private. To know Rosa Luxemburg as scientist and protagonist is to know only certain aspects of her complex nature. The letters from prison round off the portrait. The followers and fellow combatants of Rosa Luxemburg have every right to acquaint themselves with the wealth of thoughts and emotions that emanated from her big heart. It is good that they should see how this woman, undaunted by her own sufferings, brought a deep sympathy and a poet's vision to her understanding of all things in nature; how her heart responded to the music of bird songs; how she took a sincere interest in all the doings of her friends, in both small things and great. *We* merely point to the monument that the departed herself erected.

THE PUBLISHERS

ALL THE LETTERS CONTAINED IN THIS COLLECTION WERE ADDRESSED TO MRS. SOPHIE LIEBKNECHT

An den Pflaster-
steinen interessierten mich die bunten
Farben: rötlich, bläulich, grün, grau.
Namentlich in dem langen Winter,
der so sehr auf ein bischen lebendiges
Grün warten liess, haben meine
farbenhungrigen Augen sich an den
Steinen ein wenig Buntheit u. Anre-
gung zu schaffen gesucht. Und jetzt,
wo Sommer ist, da gab es zwischen
den Steinen soviel Eigenartiges und

FROM LEIPZIG

(A postcard) *)

Leipzig, July 7, 1916.

My dear little Sonya,[1])

The heat is steamy and oppressive, as it so often is in Leipzig — I find the weather here very trying. This morning I sat for two hours beside the pond in the park, reading *The Man of Property* [2]).

It's brilliant. A little old woman sat down beside me, glanced at the titlepage, and smiled, saying: "That must be a fine book. I am fond of reading myself". Before I settled down to read, of course I had a good look at the trees and shrubs in the park, and was glad to see that they were all old friends. It is quite different with human beings, for I find that contact with them grows continually more unsatisfying: I think I shall retire into a hermitage, like St. Antony — minus the temptations! Try not to worry.

With much love,

Rosa

Love to the children.

*) Rosa Luxemburg was arrested on July 10th. This postcard is the only one written while the author was still at liberty.

FROM BERLIN

(A postcard)

Berlin, August 5, 1916.
(The prison in the Barnimstrasse)

✓ My dear little Sonya.

To-day, August 5th, I have just received your two letters; they came together, the one of July 11th (! !) and the one of July 23rd.

You see that the post works more slowly than if I were in New York. But the books you sent me came to hand earlier. Heartfelt thanks for everything. I am so sorry that I had to leave you in your present situation; how I should have liked to stroll with you through the fields once more, or watch the sunset from the bay-window in your kitchen. . . . Helmi [3]), too, sent me a long postcard describing his journey. Thanks so much also for the Hölderlin [4]). But you must not squander so much money on me; I really don't like it.

Thanks so much for the hamper of good things and for the beans.

Write soon, for then perhaps I shall get another letter before the end of the month. Warmest love. Keep your heart up. You are never out of my thoughts. Much love to Karl and the children.

Your

Rosa

The Pierre Loti [5]) is splendid; I havn't read the other books yet.

FROM WRONKE[6]

(A postcard)[7]

Wronke, August 24, 1916.

Dear Sonichka.

It grieves me so much that I cannot be with you at this moment. But be brave; there will soon be a turn for the better.

The main thing is that you should have a change — no matter where you go, so long as it is in the country where everything is fresh and lovely, and where you will be properly looked after. You would be foolish to stay where you are and mope. It is likely to be many weeks before the appeal can be heard. Do get away as soon as you possibly can . . . Karl will certainly be easier in his mind when he knows that you are in the country. A thousand thanks for your letter of the 10th and for your sendings. Certainly we shall all be together next spring, having country walks or strolling through the Botanical Gardens, and I love to look forward to it. But for the present, Sonichka, you must have a change. Can't you manage to go to Lake Constance, to get a breath of southern air? But I must see you before you go. Write to the Governor for leave. Let me have another line from you soon. Make your mind as easy as you can.

Fondest love.

R.

Send my most affectionate greetings to Karl.
I was delighted to get Helmi's and Bobbi's cards.

Wronke, November 21, 1916.

My dear little Sonichka,

I hear from Mathilde that your brother has been killed at the front. The idea that you have this fresh blow to endure is a great shock to me. Lately there has been one trouble after another.

And yet I cannot be with you, to cheer you up a little! . . . I am uneasy, too, at the thought of your mother, wondering how she will bear this new sorrow. These are sad days, and all of us have lost many of our loved ones. As during the siege of Sebastopol, every month seems a year. I do hope I shall be able to see you soon, for I am longing to do so. How did you hear about your brother; through your mother, or direct? What news of your other brother?

I did so much want to send you something by Mathilde, and I had absolutely nothing but the little coloured kerchief; don't make fun of it; I only sent it to show that I love you. Write a line or two as soon as you can, to let me know you are all right.

Love to Karl and your dear self.

Your

Rosa

Much love to the children.

Wronke, January 15, 1917.

. . . . . . I felt my position keenly for a moment to-day. The whistle of the engine at 3.19 told me that Mathilde was leaving. Like a beast in a cage I positively ran to and fro along the wall where I usually "go for a walk". My heart throbbed with pain as I said to myself, "If only I too could get away from here, *if only I too could get away!*". Oh, well, this heart of mine has become like a well trained dog; I gave it a slap and told it to lie down.

Enough of me and my troubles.

Sonichka, do you remember what we settled to do as soon as the war is over, how we decided to go to the south. We'll keep to that plan. I know your fancy is to go with me to Italy, the goal of your desire.

My plan is to carry you off to Corsica. That is even finer than Italy. In Corsica one can forget Europe, or at any rate modern Europe. Picture to yourself a vast landscape in the heroic style, mountains and valleys sharply cut; above, nothing but bare masses of lovely grey rock; below luxuriant olive groves, cherry-laurels, and venerable Spanish chestnut trees. Over all there broods a primeval stillness.

There is neither voice of man nor song of bird, only the ripple of a streamlet as it courses down its stony bed, or the murmur of the wind through the fissures in the rocks overhead—still the same wind that bellied the sail of Odysseus. Such human beings as you do meet are in perfect accord with the landscape. Round a turn of the mountain path there will suddenly appear some peasants walking in Indian file, for the Corsicans never go about in groups like our peasants.

Usually a dog leads the way; then at a slow march comes a goat perhaps, or a donkey laden with sacks full of chestnuts; next a great mule, on which sits a woman sideways, her legs hanging straight down, a child in her arms; she is bolt upright, slender as a cypress, and makes no movement. Beside her strides a bearded man whose demeanour is calm and confident. Both are silent. You would take your oath that they are the Holy Family. Such a scene is frequently to be witnessed. Everytime I was so profoundly stirred that involuntarily I wanted to kneel, which is always my inclination when I see anything perfectly beautiful. There the Bible is still a living reality, and so is the classical world.

We must go, and just in the way I went. We must wander all over the island, sleeping every night in a different place, and always afoot to greet the sunrise. Does not that tempt you? I should love to introduce you to this new world . . . . .

Keep up your reading, you must go on with your mental training, and it will be quite easy for you since your mind is still fresh and pliable. No more to-day. Be cheerful and serene.

Your Rosa

Wronke, February 18, 1917.

. . . . . It is long since I have been shaken by anything as by Martha's brief report of your visit to Karl, how you had to see him through a grating, and the impression it made on you. Why didn't you tell me about it? I have a right to share in anything which hurts you, and I wouldn't allow anyone to curtail my proprietary rights!

Besides, Martha's account reminded me so vividly of the first time my brother and my sister came to see me ten years ago in the Warsaw citadel. There they put you in a regular cage consisting of two layers of wire mesh; or rather, a small cage stands freely inside a larger one, and the prisoner only sees the visitor through this double trellis-work. It was just at the end of a six-day hunger strike, and I was so weak that the Commanding Officer of the fortress had almost to carry me into the visitors' room. I had to hold on with both hands to the wires of the cage, and this must certainly have strengthened the resemblance to a wild beast in the Zoo. The cage was standing in a rather dark corner of the room, and my brother pressed his face against the wires. "Where are you?", he kept on asking, continually wiping away the tears that clouded his glasses. — How glad I should be if I could only take Karl's place in the cage of Luckau prison, so as to save him from such an ordeal!

Convey my most grateful thanks to Pfemfert for Galsworthy's book. I finished it yesterday, and liked it so much. Not as much as *The Man of Property.* It pleased me less, precisely because in it social criticism is more preponderant. When I am reading a novel I am less concerned with any moral it may convey than with its purely artistic merits. What troubles me in the case of *Fraternity* is that Galsworthy's *intelligence* overburdens the book. This criticism will surprise you. I regard Galsworthy as of the same type as Bernard Shaw and Oscar Wilde, a type which now has many representatives among the British intelligentsia. They are able, ultra-civilised, a trifle bored with the world, and they are inclined to regard everything with a humorous scepticism. The subtly ironical remarks that Galsworthy makes concerning his own *dramatis personae* remaining himself apparently quite serious the while, often make me burst out laughing. But persons who are truly well bred, rarely or never make fun of their own associates, even though they do not fail to note anything ludicrous; in like manner, a supreme artist never makes a butt of his own creations.

Don't misunderstand me, Sonichka; don't think that I am objecting to satire in the grand style! For example, Gerhart Hauptmann's[8]) *Emanuel Quint* is the most ferocious satire of modern society that has been written for a hundred years. But the author himself is not on the grin as he writes. At the close he stands with lips atremble, and the tears glisten in his widely open eyes. Galsworthy, on the other hand, with his smartly-phrased interpolations, makes me feel as I have felt at an evening party when my neighbour, as each new guest has entered, has whispered some appropriate piece of spite into my ear . . . .

This is Sunday, the deadliest of days for prisoners and solitaries. I am sad at heart, but I earnestly hope that both you and Karl are free from care. Write soon to let me know when and where you are at length going for a change.

All my love to you and the children.

Your Rosa

Do you think Pfemfert could send me something else worth reading? Perhaps one of Thomas Mann's[9]) books? I have not read any of them yet.

One more request. I am beginning to find the sun rather trying when I go out; could you send me a yard of black spotted veiling?

Thanks in advance.

Wronke, April 19. 1917.

Your card yesterday gave me a great deal of pleasure, although it was rather melancholy. If only I could be with you now to make you laugh once more as I did that time after Karl's arrest. Do you remember how we made everyone stare at us by the way we were laughing in the *Café Fürstenhof*? We had a jolly time, then, in spite of everything. Think how we used to drive in a motor car down *Potsdamer Platz* every morning, and on to the prison across the *Tiergarten* where the flowers were blooming, through the quiet *Lehrter Strasse* with its tall elms; then, on the way back, we made it a point of honour to get out at the *Fürstenhof;* after that, you had always to come to my place in the South End, where everything was in its May glory; next came the pleasant hours in my kitchen, where you and my little Mimi sat patiently waiting the achievements of my culinary skill. (Do you remember those runner beans I cooked after the French manner?)

Through all my memories of the time runs a vivid impression of the persistently brilliant and hot weather, the only sort of weather that gives a really joyful sense of spring.

In the evening, of course I had to visit you in my turn, to go to your dear little room. — I love you as a housewife, it suits you to perfection, standing at the table with your girlish figure, as you pour out the tea. Finally, towards midnight we used to see one another home through the dimly lighted, flower-scented streets. Can you recall that wonderful moonlit night in the South End, when I saw you home, how the gables, steeply silhouetted in black against the lovely deep blue of the night sky, resembled the battlements of feudal castles?

Sonyusha, if only I could always be with you, to take your mind off your troubles, sometimes talking and sometimes silent, so that I could keep you from unhappy brooding. In your card you ask: "Why do these things happen?" Dear child, life is like that, and always has been. Sorrow. and parting, and unsatisfied yearnings, are just a part of life. We have to take everything as it comes, and to find beauty in everything. That's what I manage to do. Not from any profound wisdom, but simply because it is my nature. I feel instinctively that this is the only right way of taking life, and that is why I am truly happy in all possible circumstances. I would not spare anything out of my life, or have it different from what it has been and is. If only I could bring you to my way of looking at things . . . . . .

But I haven't thanked you yet for Karl's photograph. I was so delighted to get it. You could not possibly have thought of a more lovely birthday present. He is on the table in a fine frame and his eyes follow me about wherever I go. (You know how the eyes in some pictures seem to be looking at one wherever one is.) The likeness is excellent. How pleased Karl must be at the news from Russia. But you have good reason to rejoice too, for now there is nothing to hinder your mother

2*

from coming to see you. Had you thought of that? For your sake I do so long for sunshine and warmth. Here the buds have not opened yet, and yesterday we had sleet. How far is the spring advanced in my "southern landscape" in the South End of Berlin? Last year at this time we were standing together at the garden gate and you were admiring the wealth of flowers . . . .

Don't trouble about writing. I shall often write to you, but I shall be quite satisfied if you send me a postcard now and then.

Have you got my little Botanist's Guide with you? Don't worry, darling; everything will come out all right, you'll see.

Much love.

Always your

Rosa

Wronke, May 2, 1917.

. . . . Do you remember how, in April last year, I called you up on the telephone at ten in the morning to come at once to the Botanical Gardens and listen to the nightingale which was giving a regular concert there? We hid ourselves in a thick shrubbery, and sat on the stones beside a trickling streamlet. When the nightingale had ceased singing, there suddenly came a plaintive, monotonous cry that sounded something like "Gligligligligliglick!" I said I thought it must be some kind of marsh bird, and Karl agreed; but we never learned exactly what bird it was. Just fancy, I heard the same call suddenly *here* from somewhere close at hand a few days ago in the early morning, and I burned with impatience to find out what the bird was. I could not rest until I had done so. It is not a marsh bird after all.

It is a *wryneck*, a grey bird, larger than a sparrow. It gets its name because of the way in which, when danger threatens, it tries to intimidate its enemies by quaint gestures and writhings of the neck. It lives only on ants, collecting them with its sticky tongue, just like an ant-eater. The Spaniards call it *hormiguero,* — the ant-bird. Mörike[10]) has written some amusing verses on the wryneck, and Hugo Wolf[11]) has set them to music. Now that I've found out what bird it is that gave the plaintive cry, I am so pleased as if some one had given me a present. You might write to Karl about it, he will like to know.

You ask what I am reading. Natural science for the most part; I am studying the distribution of plants and animals.

Yesterday I was reading about the reasons for the disappearance of song birds in Germany. The spread of scientific forestry, horticulture, and agriculture, have cut them off from their nesting places and their food supply. More and more, with modern methods, we are doing away with hollow trees, waste lands, brushwood, fallen leaves. I felt sore at heart. I was not thinking so much about the loss of pleasure for human beings, but I was so much distressed at the idea of the stealthy and inexorable destruction of these defenceless little creatures, that the tears came into my eyes. I was reminded of a book I read in Zurich, in which Professor Sieber describes the dying-out of the Redskins in North America. Just like the birds, they have been gradually driven from their hunting grounds by civilised men.

I suppose I must be out of sorts to feel everything so deeply. Sometimes, however, it seems to me that I am not really a human being at all but like a bird or a beast in human form. I feel so much more at home even in a scrap of garden like the one here, and still more in the meadows when the grass is humming with bees than — at one of our party congresses. I can say that to you, for you will not promptly suspect me of treason to socialism! You know that I really hope to die at my post, in a street fight or in prison.

But my innermost personality belongs more to my tomtits than to the comrades. This is not because, like so many spiritually bankrupt politicians, I seek refuge and find repose in nature. Far from it, in nature at every turn I see so much cruelty that I suffer greatly.

Take the following episode, which I shall never forget. Last spring I was returning from a country walk when, in the quiet, empty road, I noticed a small dark patch on the ground. Leaning forward I witnessed a voiceless tragedy. A large beetle was lying on its back and waving its legs helplessly, while a crowd of little ants were swarming round it and eating it alive! I was horror stricken, so I took my pocket handkerchief and began to flick the little brutes away. They were so bold and stubborn that it took me some time, and when at length I had freed the poor wretch of a beetle and had carried it to a safe distance on the grass, two of its legs had already been gnawed off . . .

I fled from the scene feeling that in the end I had conferred a very doubtful boon.

The evening twilight lasts so long now. I love this hour of the gloaming. In the South End I had plenty of blackbirds, but here there are none to be seen or heard. I was feeding a pair all through the winter, but they have vanished.

In the South End I used to stroll through the streets at this hour. It always fascinates me when, during the last violet gleam of daylight, the ruddy gas lamps suddenly flash out, still looking so strange in the half light as if they were almost ashamed of themselves. Then one sees indistinctly a figure moving swiftly through the street, perhaps a servant maid hastening to fetch something from the baker or the grocer before the shops close. The bootmaker's children, who are friends of mine, used to go on playing in the streets after dark, until a loud call summoned them in. And there was always a belated blackbird which could not settle down, but like a naughty child would go on wailing, or would wake with a start and fly noisily from tree to tree.

For my part, I would continue standing in the middle of the street numbering the stars as they came out, reluctant to go home, unwilling to leave the mild air, and the twilight in which day and night were so gently caressing one another.

Sonyusha, I will write again soon. Make your mind easy, everything will turn out all right, for Karl too. Good-bye till the next letter.

With love

Your Rosa

Wronke, May 19, 1917.

. . . . . . It is so lovely here now! Everything is green and burgeoning. The foliage of the horse-chestnuts is resplendent; the currant bushes are covered with clusters of yellow stars; the cherry tree, with its reddish leaves, is already in flower; and the black alder will soon blossom.

Louise Kautsky visited me to-day. As a parting gift she gave me some forget-me-nots and some pansies. They've all settled themselves in so nicely; I can hardly believe my eyes, for this is the first time in my life I ever did any planting out. By Whitsuntide I shall have such a lot of flowers under my window!

There is a great variety of newly arrived birds here now.

Hardly a day passes without my making acquaintance with a bird I have never seen before. By the way, you remember that morning in the Botanical Gardens with Karl when we were listening to the nightingale. We saw a huge tree whose leaves were not yet showing, but it was covered with small white flowers; we were all puzzled what it could be, for obviously it was not a fruit tree, and the flowers were quite unfamiliar. I know now! It was a white poplar, and what we thought were flowers were not flowers at all but young leaves. The fully grown leaf of the white poplar is white only on the under surface, whilst the upper surface is dark green; but the young leaves are still covered on both sides with white down, and they shine in the sunlight like flowers.

There is a huge white poplar in my garden. and all the song birds like this tree the best. That same day both of you came to see me in the evening; do you remember? We had such a lovely time, reading aloud to one another. Towards midnight, when we were standing saying goodbye (such a delightful breeze laden with the odour of jasmine came in trough the window opening on the verandah) I recited to you the Spanish song of which I am so fond:

Be praise to him through whom these worlds arose!
How wonderful he made this span increasing!
He made the ocean's endless deep repose,
He made the ships that pass across unceasing,
He made yon paradise of calmed radiance,
He made the Earth, dear — and thy countenance.

Sonitchka, if you have never heard that sung to the accompaniment of Wolf's music, you cannot imagine the intensity of passion in those two concluding words.

As I write, a great humble-bee has flown into the room, and fills it with a diapason tone. How lovely it is; how keen the joy of life conveyed by this rich note, vibrant with energy, summer heat and the scent of flowers.

Cheer up, Sonitchka, and write to me soon, soon; I am longing to hear from you.

Your Rosa

Wronke, May 23, 1917.

Your last letter, the one of May 14th, had already reached the prison when I sent mine to the pöst. I am so glad to be in touch with you again, and to-day I want to send you a cordial Whitsuntide greeting.

You remember the opening words of Goethe's[12]) *Reynard the Fox:* "Whitsuntide, the joyous festival had come." I do hope you will pass a cheerful Whitsuntide. Last year at this season we made with Mathilde that delightful excursion to Lichtenrade, where I picked the bundle of long grasses for Karl and the exquisite spray of birch catkins.

In the evening we went for another walk through the fields at the South End, with roses in our hands like the "three noblewomen of Ravenna" . . . . The lilac is in bloom here, the buds opened to-day; it is so warm, that I have begun to wear my thinnest summer dress.

Notwithstanding the sunshine and the heat, my little birds have almost stopped singing. They are too busy to think of anything but their eggs, the hens are sitting, and the cocks have their beaks full seeking food for themselves and their mates. Besides, I suppose their nests are in the open country or in the big trees. At any rate all is quiet in my little garden, except that now and again the nightingale sings a note or two, or the greenfinch makes a rat-tat-tat with its feet, or perhaps the chaffinch sounds its pipe late in the evening. My tits are no longer to be seen. Yesterday, indeed, I had a brief greeting, of a sudden, from a blue-tit; the sound came from a long way off, and thrilled me more than you can imagine. For the blue-tit, you know, is not like the coal-tit a bird that stays with us all the winter; it only comes back towards the end of March. At first this blue-tit used to fly about quite close to my window. It came to the sill with the others, and diligently sang its merry "zeezeebey", a long-drawn-out call, reminding one of a mischievous child in a teasing mood. It always made me laugh, and answer with the same phrase. Then the bird vanished with the others in the beginning of this month, nesting no doubt elsewhere. I had seen and heard nothing of it for weeks. Yesterday its well-known notes came suddenly from the other side of the wall which separates our courtyard from another part of the prison; but it was considerably altered, for the bird shrilled thrice in brief succession "zeezeebey, zeezeebey. zeezeebey", and then all was still. It went to my heart, for there was so much conveyed by this hasty call from the distance — a whole history of bird life. There was a reminiscence of the splendid days of wooing in the spring, when the birds could sing and make love the livelong day; now the blue-tit had to be on the wing all the time collecting flies for itself and the family. The bird seemed to be saying: "I've no time to spare; oh how lovely it was; spring is nearly over; zeezeebey, zeezeebey, zeezeebey!"

Will you believe me, Sonyusha, when I tell you that a little snatch of bird song can be so full of meaning, can move me so profoundly. My mother, who considered that Schiller[13]) and the Bible were the supreme sources of wisdom, was firmly convinced that King Solomon understood the language of birds. In the pride of my fourteen years and my training in natural science I used to smile at my mother's simplicity. But now I have myself grown to be like King Solomon; I too can understand the language of birds and beasts. Not, of course, as if they were using articulate speech, but I understand the most varied shades of meaning and of feeling conveyed by their tones. Only to the rude ear of one who is quite indifferent, does the song of a bird seem always the same. Those who love birds and beasts, those who have a sympathetic understanding, can perceive great diversity of expression, and can recognise a complete language. There is a meaning even in the universal silence which has followed the clamour of the early spring. I know that if I am still here in the autumn (as I probably shall be) all my friends will come back to seek food at my window. Already I can rejoice at the return of this blue-tit which is a special friend of mine.

Sonyusha, you are feeling embittered because of my long imprisonment. You ask: "How can human beings dare to decide the fate of their fellows? What is the meaning of it all?" You won't mind — I couldn't help laughing as I read. In Dostoyeffsky's[14]) novel, *The Brothers Karamazoff*, one of the characters, Madame Hokhlakova, used to ask the same questions; she would look round from one member of the company to another, and would then blurt out a second question before there had been time to begin an answer to the first. My dear little bird. the whole history of civilisation (which according to a modest estimate extends through some twenty thousand years) is grounded upon "human beings deciding the fate of their fellows"; the practice is deeply rooted in the material conditions of existence. Nothing but a further evolution, and a painful one, can change such things. At this hour we are living in the very chapter of the transition, and you ask "What is the meaning of it all?" Your query is not a reasonable one to make concerning the totality of life and its forms. Why are there blue-tits in the world? I really don't know, but I'm glad that there are, and it is sweet to me when a hasty "zeezeebey" sounds suddenly from beyond the wall.

Moreover, you make too much of my "equanimity". My poise and my cheerfulness can, alas, be disturbed by the slightest of shadows. When that happens, I suffer inexpressibly, but it is my way to suffer in silence. Literally, Sonichka, I am unable at such times to utter a word. For example, within these last few days, I was feeling so bright and cheerful, rejoicing in the sunshine. Then, on Monday, there came a piercing wind, and in an instant my radiant spirits gave way to the profoundest gloom.

If at this moment the very joy of my soul had stood embodied before me, I should have been unable to utter a word of greeting, and could only have gazed at the vision in a dumb despair. In fact I rarely have much inclination to talk. Weeks pass without my hearing the sound of my own voice. This is why I heroically resolved not to have my little Mimi here. She is used to cheerfulness and bustle; she is pleased when I sing, laugh.

and play hide-and-seek with her all over the house; she would be hipped here. That is why I have left her in Mathilde's care. Mathilde is coming to visit me in a few days, and that will cheer me up. Perhaps for me, too, Whitsuntide will be "the joyous festival". But Sonichka, you must not get into the dumps yourself; I know everything will turn out all right in the end. Give my love to Karl. A good hug to yourself.

Your Rosa

Many thanks for the charming picture.

End of May 1917.

Sonyusha,

Where do you think I am writing this letter? In the garden! I have brought out a small table at which I am now seated, hidden among the shrubs. To the right is the currant bush, smelling of cloves; to the left, a privet in flower; overhead, a sycamore and a young slender Spanish chestnut stretch their broad, green hands; in front is the tall, serious and gentle white poplar, its silvery leaves rustling in the breeze.

On the paper, as I write, the faint shadows of the leaves are at play with the interspersed patches of sunlight; the foliage is still damp from a recent shower, and now and again drops fall on my face and hands.

Service is going on in the prison chapel; the sound of the organ reaches me indistinctly, for it is masked by the noise of the leaves, and by the clear chorus of the birds, which are all in a merry mood to-day; from afar I hear the call of the cuckoo.

How lovely it is; I am so happy. One seems already to have the Midsummer mood — the full luxuriance of summer and the intoxication of life. Do you remember the scenes in Wagner's[15]) *Meistersinger*, the one in which the prentices sing "Midsummer Day! Midsummer Day!", and the folk scene where, after singing "St. Crispin! St. Crispin!" the motley crowd joins in a frolicsome dance?

Such days as these are well fitted to produce the mood of those scenes.

I had *such* an experience yesterday. I must tell you what happened. In the bathroom, before dinner, I found a great peacock-butterfly on the window. It must have been shut up there for two or three days, for it had almost worn itself out fluttering against the hard windowpane, so that there was now nothing more than a slight movement of the wings to show that it was still alive.

Directly I noticed it, I dressed myself, trembling with impatience, climbed up to the window, and took it cautiously in my hand. It had now ceased to move, and I thought it must be dead. But I took it to my own room and put it on the outside window sill, to see if it would revive. There was again a gentle fluttering for a little, but after that the insect did not move. I laid a few flowers in front of its antennae, so that it might have something to eat. At that moment the black-cap sang in front of the window so lustily that the echoes rang. Involuntarily I spoke out loud to the butterfly, saying: "Just listen how merrily the bird is singing; you must take heart, too, and come to life again!" I could not help laughing at myself for speaking like this to a half-dead butterfly, and I thought: "You are wasting your breath!" But I was not, for in about half an hour the little creature really revived; after moving about for a while, it was able to flutter slowly away. I was so delighted at this rescue. In the afternoon, of course, I went out into the garden again. I am there always from eight in the morning till noon, when

3

I am summoned to dinner; and again from three till six.

I was expecting the sun to shine, for I felt that it must really show itself once more. But the sky was overcast, and I grew melancholy.

I strolled about the garden. A light breeze was blowing, and I saw a remarkable sight. The over ripe catkins on the white poplar were scattered abroad; their seed-down was carried in all directions, filling the air as if with snow-flakes, covering the ground and the whole courtyard; the silvery seed-down made everything look quite ghostlike. The white poplar blooms later than the catkin-bearing trees, and spreads far and wide thanks to this luxuriant dispersal of its seeds; the young shoots sprout like weeds from all the crannies on the wall and from between the paving stones.

At six o'clock, as usual, I was locked up. I sat gloomily by the window with a dull sense of oppression in the head, for the weather was sultry. Looking upward I could see at a dizzy hight the swallows flying gaily to and fro against a background formed of white, fleecy clouds in a pastel-blue sky; their pointed wings seemed to cut the air like scissors.

Soon the heavens were overcast, everything became blurred; there was a thunder storm with torrents of rain, and two loud peals of thunder which shook the whole place. I shall never forget what followed. The storm had passed on; the sky had turned a thick monotonous grey; a pale, dull, spectral twilight suddenly diffused itself over the landscape, so that it seemed as if the whole prospect were under a thick grey veil. A gentle rain was falling steadily upon the leaves; sheet lightning flamed at brief intervals, tinting the leaden grey with flashes of purple, while the distant thunder could still be heard rumbling like the declining waves of a heavy sea. Then, quite abruptly, the nightingale began to sing in the sycamore in front of my window.

Despite the rain, the lightning and the thunder, the notes rang out as clear as a bell. The bird sang as if intoxicated, as if possessed, as if wishing to drown the thunder, to illuminate the twilight.

Never have I heard anything so lovely. On the background of the alternately leaden and lurid sky, the song seemed to show like shafts of silver. It was so mysterious, so incredibly beautiful, that involuntarily I murmured the last verse of Goethe's poem,

"Oh, wert thou here!"

Always your

Rosa

Wronke, June 1, 1917.

. . . . . . I know the different kinds of orchids well. I studied them once for several days in the wonderful hothouses at Frankfort-on-the-Main, where a whole section is filled with them. It was after the trial in which I was sentenced to one year's imprisonment.

Their slender grace and their fantastic, almost unnatural forms make them seem to me over-refined and decadent. They produce on me the impression of a dainty marquise of the powder-and-patch period.

The admiration I feel for them has to encounter an internal resistance, and is attended with a certain uneasiness, for by disposition I am antagonistic to everything decadent and perverse. A common dandelion gives me far more pleasure. It has so much sunshine in its colour; like me, it expands gratefully in the sun, and furls its petals shyly at the least shade.

What lovely evenings and what glorious nights we are having now! Yesterday everything seemed under the influence of an indescribable charm. Long after the sun had set, huge rays of a vague but brilliant tint — a sort of opal — were still spreading across the sky; it looked like a huge palette upon which a painter had squeezed the colour out of his brushes after a long day's work.

The atmosphere was sultry; there was a slight feeling of tension, producing a sense of oppression; the shrubs were motionless, the nightingale was silent, but the indefatigable black-cap was still hopping from twig to twig uttering its clear call. There was a general feeling of expectation. I stood at the window and waited too, though I haven't the slightest idea what I was waiting for. After "closing time" at six I have nothing more to expect betwixt heaven and earth.

Wronke, July 20, 1917.

Sonichka,

My darling, since my stay here has been longer than I expected, you shall have one more greeting from Wronke. How could you possibly think I was not going to write to you any more? There has been no change, there can be none, in my feeling towards you. The reason why I have not written for some time is because I knew that since leaving Ebenhausen you must have had a thousand things to think of, but in part also because I was not in a letter writing mood.

You must have heard, I think, that I am to be transferred to Breslau. I said farewell to my little garden this morning. The weather is grey and stormy; rain threatens, and clouds are racing through the sky; but still I was able to enjoy my customary morning walk.

I took leave of the narrow, paved path along the wall, where I have paced to and fro for nearly nine months now, so that I know every stone and all the weeds that grow in the crevices of the paving. I like the motley colouring of these stones, reddish and bluish, grey and green.

Especially during the long winter, when one has such a craving for something that is green and growing, my eyes that were hungry for colour dwelt gladly on these stones, to enjoy the stimulus of their varied tints. As soon as the summer came, there was so much of interest to be studied in the crannies. Wild bees and wasps make their homes here in great numbers. They bore holes about the size of a walnut, and excavate long passages underground, carrying the earth to the surface, where they make lovely little heaps. In the underground galleries they lay their eggs and store wax and wild honey. All day they are flying in and out so busily. When walking there I have to be most careful to avoid shaking their subterranean dwellings. Then there are several places where the ants have highways along which they move in endless processions, in such perfectly straight lines that one feels that they must have an instinctive knowledge of the mathematical definition that a straight line is the shortest way between two points (a fact of which primitive man was quite unaware!).

On the wall, weeds flourish. Side by side with some that have withered, are others still sprouting indefatigably. There has also been a whole generation of young trees that have shot up this spring under my very eyes, growing either from the earth in the middle of the path or from the crevices in the wall. For instance, there is a little acacia, obviously a fallen shoot from the old tree. There are several small white poplars; they only came into the world last May, but they already display a luxuriant whitish-green foliage which waves gracefully in the wind just like that of the parent tree. How many times I have paced up and down here, how much I have felt and thought! In the severe winter, when snow had just fallen, I had often to break a trail for myself, accompanied always by my favourite little coal-tit, which I had hoped to see again next autumn, but which will not find me when it comes to its old feeding ground at the window. In March, when the frost broke for a few days, my path became a watery channel. A warm wind was blowing; it made little waves on the surface of the water, but at other times the wall was mirrored in the pools. At length May came, and with it those first violets on the wall, the ones I sent you.

To-day, when I was walking, looking, and thinking, some lines of Goethe's were running in my head:

Old Merlin in his shining grave,
Where in my youth I spoke to him. . . .

You know what follows. Of course the poem had no bearing on my mood or upon the things I was thinking of. It was merely the music of the words and the rare charm of the verses which exercised a lulling influence. I don't know why it is that a beautiful poem, especially one of Goethe's, always seems to exercise so powerful an influence upon me. At times of profound agitation the effect is almost physiological, as if when parched with thirst I had been given a precious drink to cool my body and restore my mind. I don't know the poem from the *Westöstliche Diwan*[10]) to which you refer in your last letter; you might copy it out for me. Another poem which I have been wanting for a long time, for it is not to be found in the volume of Goethe I have with me, is *Blumengruss*[11]). It is quite a short poem consisting of four to six lines. I know it as one of Wolf's songs which is exquisitely beautiful. As far as I can remember, the last stanza runs as follows:

42

I have gathered them
With an ardent yearning;
I have pressed them to my heart
A thousand, thousand times.

In the music there is something so holy, so delicate, so pure, that it is like kneeling in silent prayer. I have forgotten the exact words and should like to have them.

About nine yesterday evening I had a glorious sight. When I was lying on the sofa I noticed a pink glow reflected from the window, which surprised me, for the sky was overcast. I ran to the window and was fascinated at what I saw. On the background of the monotonously grey sky, there towered in the east a huge cloud of an amazingly beautiful rose colour; it was so detached from its surroundings that it looked like a smile, like a greeting from afar. I breathed with a sense of renewed freedom, and involuntarily stretched out both hands towards the enchanting vision. Surely when there are such colours and such forms, life is lovely, life is worth living? I drank deep draughts of this rosy radiance, until in the end I felt that I must laugh at myself. After all, the sky and the clouds and the varied beauties of life are to be seen in other places than this, and I shall not take leave of them when I quit Wronke. They come with me, they will be with me wherever I may be and as long as I may live.

I shall send you a line from Breslau before long. Come to see me there as soon as you can. Best love to Karl and to yourself. Farewell till we meet in my new prison.

Your own

Rosa

43

FROM BRESLAU [18)]

Breslau, August 2, 1917.

My dear Sonichka,

Your letter, which reached me on the 28th, was my first news here from the outer world; so you can readily imagine how glad I was to get it. Your affectionate anxiety on my account makes you take too tragical a view of my removal. . . . You know that I accept all the turns of fortune with a fair amount of equanimity. I have already settled in here quite comfortably. My book boxes turned up to-day from Wronke, so it wouldn't be long now before the books, the pictures, and the modest ornaments that I like to carry about with me, will make my two cells at Breslau just as homelike and comfortable as were my quarters at Wronke, so that I shall be able to resume my work with renewed pleasure. Of course I lack here the comparative freedom of movement I had at Wronke, where during the day I could go wherever I liked within the fortress. Here I am simply locked up, minus the glorious fresh air, the garden, and, above all, the birds. You can't think how much I had come to depend on the society of those little creatures. Still, one can soon learn to do without things, and before long I shall forget that I was ever in better surroundings than these. The whole position here is much like that of the *Barnimstrasse*, except that there I had the lovely green infirmary garden in which every day I could make some new little discovery in botany or zoology. There is no chance of "discovering" anything in the great paved courtyard where I take exercise. As I go to and fro, I keep my eyes riveted on the grey paving-stones to spare myself the sight of the prisoners at work in the yard. It hurts me to see them in their ignoble prison dress, and there are always a few among them in whom the individual traits of age and sex seem to have been obliterated beneath an imprint of the extremity of human degradation — — — and yet these very figures always draw my gaze by a painful sort of magnetism. It is true that there are others upon whom prison dress can wreak no ill, and who would rejoice the eye of any painter. For instance, I have seen a young working woman in the courtyard here whose slender trim figure, and whose sharply-cut profile set off by the kerchief she wears on her head, remind me of one of Millet's[19]) peasant women. It is a delight to watch the grace with which she carries burdens. Her thin face, with its tightly-drawn skin and its uniform pallor, recalls the tragical mask of a pierrot. But I have been taught by painful experience to shun such promising encounters as widely as possible. In the *Barnimstrasse* there was a prisoner whose aspect was queenly, and I fancied that her personality must fit the part. Shortly afterwards she took up the duties of cleaner in my section of the prison, and within a day or two it became plain to me that her lovely mask hid such a mass of stupidity and baseness that I had to turn away my eyes whenever she crossed my path. It occured to me, in this connection, that it may only be because the Venus of Milo[20]) cannot speak that she has been able for all these years to preserve her reputation as the most beautiful among women. Were she to open her mouth maybe the spell would be broken.

My window looks upon the men's prison, the usual gloomy building of red brick. But over the wall I can see the green tree-tops belonging to some kind of park. One of them is a tall black poplar which I can hear rustling when the wind is strong; and there is a row of ash trees, much lighter in colour, and covered with yellow clusters of seed-pods. The windows look to the north-west, so that I often see splendid sunsets. and you know how the sight of these rose-tinted clouds can make up to me for everything. At eight o'clock in the evening (summer time, 7 o'clock really) the sun has only just sunk behind the gables of the men's prison; it still shines right through the dormer-windows, and the whole sky has a golden tint. I feel so happy then, and something — I know not what — makes me hum Gounod's[21]) *Ave Maria* (you know it of course). Many thanks for copying out the Goethe poems. *Die berechtigten Maenner* is really very fine, although I had never been struck by it before; we are all open to suggestions in our judgments of the beautiful. If you have time, I wish you would copy out for me *Anakreons Grab*[22]). Do you know it well? Hugo Wolf's setting first enabled me really to understand it. The music gives it an architectonic character, calling up the vision of a Greek temple.

I stopped writing for a little, to watch the sunset. The sun has quite disappeared behind the buildings opposite. High in the heavens, myriads of cloudlets have assembled from somewhere; their edges have a silvery sheen; whilst the rest is of a delicate grey tint; the whole troop of them is moving northward. There was so much sublime indifference, so much smiling unconcern, about the cloud procession, that I could not but smile in my turn, and follow as I always do the rhythm of environing life. How, when there was such a sky to look at, could one possibly be ill-humoured or petty? If you will only remember to keep your eyes open, you will be able to be "good" without fail.

I am rather surprised that Karl wants you to send him a book on bird song. For me the song of the birds is inseparable from their life as a whole; it is the whole that interests me, rather than any detached detail. Send him a well-written book on the distribution of animals, for I am sure that will interest him. I do hope you will be able to visit me soon. Send a wire directly you get permission.

Much love,

Your Rosa

Lord ha' mercy on me! I've filled eight pages writing to you! Let it go at that. Thanks for the books.

Breslau, Mid-November, 1917.

My beloved Sonichka,

I hope soon to have a chance of sending you this letter at long last, so I hasten to take up my pen. For how long a time I have been forced to forbear my habit of talking to you — on paper at least. I am allowed to write so few letters, and I had to save up my chances for Hans D.[23]) who was expecting to hear from me. But now all is over. My last two letters to him were addressed to a dead man, and one has already been returned to me. His loss still seems incredible. But enough of this. I prefer to consider such matters in solitude. It only annoys me beyond expression when people try, as N. tried, "to break the news" to me, and to make a parade of their own grief by way of "consolation". Why should my closest friends understand me so little and hold me so cheaply as to be unable to realise that the best way in such cases is to say quickly, briefly, and simply: "He is dead"?

. . . . How I deplore the loss of all these months and years in which we might have had so many joyful hours together, notwithstanding all the horrors that are going on throughout the world. Do you know, Sonichka, the longer it lasts, and the more the infamy and monstrosity of the daily happenings surpasses all bounds, the more tranquil and more confident becomes my personal outlook. I say to myself that it is absurd to apply moral standards to the great elemental forces that manifest themselves in a hurricane, a flood, or an eclipse of the sun. We have to accept them simply as data for investigation, as subjects of study.

Manifestly, objectively considered, these are the only possible lines along which history can move, and we must follow the movement without losing sight of the main trend. I have the feeling that all this moral filth through which we are wading, this huge madhouse in which we live, may all of a sudden, between one day and the next, be transformed into its very opposite, as if by the stroke of a magician's wand; may become something stupendously great and heroic; *must* inevitable be so transformed, if only the war lasts a few years longer. . . Read Anatole France's[24]) *Les dieux ont soif*[25]). My main reason for admiring this work so much is because the author, with the insight of genius into all that is universally human, seems to say to us: "Behold, out of these petty personalities, out of these trivial commonplaces, arise, when the hour is ripe, the most titanic events and the most monumental gestures of history". We have to take everything as it comes both in social life and in private life; to accept what happens, tranquilly, comprehensively, and with a smile. I feel absolutely convinced that things will take the right turn when the war ends, or not long afterwards; but obviously we have first to pass through a period of terrible human suffering.

What I have just written reminds me of an incident I wish to tell you of, for it seems to me so poetical and so touching. I was recently reading a

49

scientific work upon the migrations of birds, a phenomenon which has hitherto seemed rather enigmatic. From this I learned that certain species, which at ordinary times live at enmity one with another (because some are birds of prey, whilst others are victims), will keep the peace during their great southward flight across the sea. Among the birds that come to winter in Egypt — come in such numbers that the sky is darkened by their flight — are, besides hawks, eagles, falcons and owls, thousands of little song birds such as larks, golden-crested wrens, and nightingales, mingling fearlessly with the great birds of prey. A "truce of God" seems to have been declared for the journey. All are striving towards the common goal, to drop, half dead from fatigue, in the land of the Nile, and subsequently to assort themselves by species and localities. Nay more, during the long flight the larger birds have been seen to carry smaller birds on their backs, for instance, cranes have passed in great numbers with a twittering freight of small birds of passage. Is not that charming?

.... In a tasteless jumble of poems I was looking at recently, I came across one by Hugo von Hoffmannsthal. As a rule I do not care for his writings, I consider them artificial, stilted, and obscure; I simply can't understand him. But this poem is an exception; it pleased me greatly and made a strong impression on me. I am sending you a copy of it, for I think you will like it too.

I am now deep in the study of geology. Perhaps you will think that must be a dry subject, but if so, you are mistaken. I am reading it with intense interest and passionate enjoyment; it opens up such wide intellectual vistas and supplies a more perfectly unified and more comprehensive conception of nature than any other science. There are so many things I should like to tell you about it, but for that we should have to have a real talk — — — taking a morning stroll together through the country at the South End, or seing one another home several times in succession on a calm moon-lit night. What are you reading now? How are you getting on with the *Lessing-Legende*[26])? I want to know everything about you. Write at once. if you can, by the same route; or, failing that, by the official route. without mentioning this letter. I am already counting the weeks till I can hope to see you here again. I suppose it will be soon after the New Year?

What news have you from Karl? When do you expect to see him? Give him a thousand greetings from me. All my love to you, my dear. dear Sonichka. Write soon and copiously.

Your Rosa

Breslau, Nov. 24, 1917.

You are mistaken in thinking that I have a prejudice against modern poets. About fifteen years ago I read Dehmel[27]) with pleasure. A prose piece of his — I cannot remember it very clearly, ***At the Deathbed of a beloved Wife***, or some such title — charmed me. I still know Arno Holz's[28]) ***Phantasus*** by heart. I used to be very fond of Johann Schlaf's[29]) ***Frühling.*** Then I broke away from these new loves, and returned to Goethe and Möricke. I don't understand Hoffmannsthal, and I know nothing of George[30]). It is true that in all of them I take somewhat amiss the combination of perfect form with the lack of a grand and noble philosophy. This cleavage between form and substance produces in me an impression of vacancy, so that the beauty of form becomes a positive irritant. As a rule they give wonderful portrayals of mood. But human beings are other things besides mood.

Sonichka, the evenings are magical now, like those of spring. I go down into the courtyard at four o'clock. Twilight has already begun, so *that* hideous prospect is veiled in a mysterious obscurity. The sky shines with a clear blue light, and in it floats the silvery moon. Every day at this time hundreds of rooks fly across the yard in a scattered flock, passing high in the air on their way back from the fields to the rookery where they spend the night. They fly with an easy stroke of wing, uttering a strange call, very different from the sharp cawing one hears when they are on hunt for food. The home-coming call is muted, and somewhat throaty. When a number of them caw like this, one after another. it suggests to my mind the picture of little tinkling balls of metal which they are throwing from one to the other in the air. They are exchanging notes concerning the day's happenings. These rooks seem to me so full of grave importance. when I watch them evening after evening as they trace their accustomed homeward path, that I feel quite a veneration for them and continue to gaze after them till the last one has vanished. Then I wander up and down in the darkness, watching the prisoners who are still busily at work in the yard as they flit to and fro like vague shadows. I rejoice that I am myself invisible, so completely alone, so free with my reveries and the stolen greetings that pass between me and the rooks — and the mellow air, with its suggestion of springtime, is so sweet to me. Then I see some of the prisoners bearing heavy pots (the soup for supper). All form up in two files, so that ten couples march into the building. I bring up the rear. In the courtyard and in the workshops the lights are gradually extinguished. As soon as I have gone in, the yard door is locked and bolted behind me — the day is ended. Notwithstanding my sorrow at the loss of Hans, I feel so calm. I am living in a world of fancy in which he is still alive. I often throw a smile to him when I think of him.

Farewell, Sonichka. I look forward so to your coming. Write soon, by the official route to begin with, and in the other way when you get a chance.

My love.

Your Rosa

4*

Breslau, Mid December, 1917.

Karl has been in Luckau prison for a year now. I have been thinking of that so often this month and of how it is just a year since you came to see me at Wronke, and gave me that lovely Christmas tree. This time I arranged to get one here, but they have brought me such a shabby little tree, with some of its branches broken off, — there's no comparison between it and yours. I'm sure I don't know how I shall manage to fix all the eight candles that I have got for it. This is my *third* Christmas under lock and key, but you needn't take it to heart. I am as tranquil and cheerful as ever. Last night I lay awake for a long time. I have to go to bed at ten, but can never get to sleep before one in the morning, so I lie in the dark, pondering many things. Last night my thoughts ran thiswise: "How strange it is that I am always in a sort of joyful intoxication, though without sufficient cause. Here I am lying in a dark cell upon a mattress hard as stone; the building has its usual churchyard quiet, so that one might as well be already entombed; through the window there falls across the bed a glint of light from the lamp which burns all night in front of the prison. At intervals I can hear faintly in the distance the noise of a passing train or close at hand the dry cough of the prison guard as in his heavy boots, he takes a few slow strides to stretch his limbs. The gride of the gravel beneath his feet has so hopeless a sound that all the weariness and futility of existence seems to be radiated thereby into the damp and gloomy night. I lie here alone and in silence, enveloped in the manifold black wrappings of darkness, tedium, unfreedom, and winter — and yet my heart beats with an immeasurable and incomprehensible inner joy, just as if I were moving in the brilliant sunshine across a flowery mead. And in the darkness I smile at life, as if I were the possessor of charm which would enable me to transform all that is evil and tragical into serenity and happiness. But when I search my mind for the cause of this joy, I find there is no cause, and can only laugh at myself." — I believe that the key to the riddle is simply life itself; this deep darkness of night is soft and beautiful as velvet, if only one looks at it in the right way. The gride of the damp gravel beneath the slow and heavy tread of the prison guard is likewise a lovely little song of life — for one who has ears to hear. At such moments I think of you, and would that I could hand over this magic key to you also. Then, at all times and in all places, you would be able to see the beauty, and the joy of life; then you also could live in the sweet intoxication, and make your way across a flowery mead. Do not think that I am offering you imaginary joys, or that I am preaching asceticism. I want you to taste all the real pleasures of the senses. My one desire is to give you in addition my inexhaustible sense of inward bliss. Could I do so, I should be at ease about you, knowing that in your passage trough life you were clad in a star-bespangled cloak which would protect you from everything petty, trivial, or harassing.

I am interested to hear of the lovely bunch of berries, black ones and reddish-violet ones you picked in *Steglitz Park*. The black berries may have been elder — of curse you know the elder berries which hang in thick and heavy clusters among fan-shaped leaves. More probably, however, they were privet, slender and graceful, upright spikes of berries, amid narrow, elongated green leaves. The reddish-violet berries, almost hidden by small leaves, must have been those of the dwarf medlar; their proper colour is red, but at this late season, when they are over-ripe and beginning to rot, they often assume a violet tinge. The leaves are like those of the myrtle, small, pointed, dark green in colour, with a leathery upper surface, but rough beneath.

Sonyusha, do you know Platen's[31]) *Verhängnisvolle Gabel?*[32]) Could you send it to me, or bring it when you come? Karl told me he had read it at home. George's poems are beautiful. Now I know where you got the verse, "And amid the rustling of ruddy corn". which you were fond of quoting when we were walking in the country. I wish you would copy out for me *The Modern Amades*[30]) when you have time. I am so fond of the poem (a knowledge of which I owe to Hugo Wolf's setting) but I have not got it here. Are you still reading the *Lessing Legende?* I have been re-reading Lange's[34]) *History of Materialism*, which I always find stimulating and invigorating. I do so hope you will read it some day.

Sonichka, dear, I had such a pang recently. In the court-yard where I walk, army lorries often arrive, laden with haversacks or old tunics and shirts from the front; sometimes they are stained with blood. They are sent to the women's cells to be mended, and then go back for use in the army. The other day one of these lorries was drawn by a team of buffaloes instead of horses. I had never seen the creatures close at hand before. They are much more powerfully built than our oxen, with flattened heads. and horns strongly recurved, so that their skulls are shaped something like a sheep's skull. They are black, and have huge, soft eyes. The buffaloes are war trophies from Rumania. The soldier-drivers said that it was very difficult to catch these animals, which had always run wild, and still more difficult to break them in to harness. They had been unmercifully flogged — on the principle of "*vae victis*"[35]). There are about a hundred head in Breslau alone. They have been accustomed to the luxuriant Rumanian pastures and have here to put up with lean and scanty fodder. Unsparingly exploited, yoked to heavy loads, they are soon worked to death. The other day a lorry came laden with sacks, so overladen indeed that the buffaloes were unable to drag it across the threshold of the gate. The soldier-driver, a brute of a fellow, belaboured the poor beasts so savagely with the butt end of his whip that the wardress at the gate, indignant at the sight, asked him if he had no compassion for animals. "No more than anyone has compassion for us men", he answered with an evil smile, and redoubled his blows. At length the buffaloes succeeded in drawing the load over the obstacle, but one of them was bleeding. You know their hide is proverbial for its thickness and toughness, but it had been torn. While the lorry was being unloaded, the beasts, which were utterly exhausted, stood perfectly still. The one that was bleeding had an expression on its black face and in its soft black eyes like that of a weeping child — one that has been severely thrashed and does not know why, nor how to escape from the torment of ill-treatment. I stood in front of the team; the beast looked at me; the tears welled from my own eyes. The suffering of a dearly loved brother could hardly have moved me more profoundly, than I was moved by my impotence in face of this mute agony. Far distant, lost for ever, were the green, lush meadows of Rumania. How different there the light of the sun, the breath of the wind; how different there the song of the birds and the melodious call of the herdsman. Instead, the hideous street, the foetid stable, the rank hay mingled with mouldy straw, the strange and terrible men — blow upon blow, and blood running from gaping wounds. Poor wretch, I am as powerless, as dumb, as yourself; I am at one with you in my pain, my weakness, and my longing.

Meanwhile the women prisoners were jostling one another as they busily unloaded the dray and carried the heavy sacks into the building. The driver, hands in pockets, was striding up and down the courtyard, smiling to himself as he whistled a popular air. I had a vision of all the splendour of war! . . .

Write soon, darling Sonichka.

Your Rosa

Never mind, my Sonyusha: you must be calm and happy all the same. Such is life, and we have to take it as it is, valiantly, heads erect, smiling ever — despite all.

Breslau, January 14, 1918.

My dearest Sonichka,

How long it is since I wrote to you. It feels like months. I don't even know whether you are back in Berlin, but I hope that these lines will be in time for your birthday. I had asked Mathilde to send you a spray of orchids from me, but now the poor dear is in hospital, so she will hardly be able to attend to my commission. But you know that I am with you in thought and feeling, and that I should like to frame you in flowers for your birthday — lilac orchids, white iris, sweet-scented hyacinths, every flower that is procurable. Perhaps next year I shall be able to bring you flowers myself on your birthday, and to go for a walk with you in the Botanical Gardens and in the country. How lovely it will be.

The temperature is at freezing point here today. But at the same time there is a gentle and refreshing spring feeling in the air; thick milk-white clouds are sailing in a deep blue sky; the sparrows are chirping gaily — one might think that the end of March had come. I am so looking forward to the spring. It is the only thing one never gets tired of, for every year that passes one seems to appreciate it better and to love it more.

You know, Sonichka, that, in the world of living things, spring, I mean the awakening to new life, begins *now*, early in January, without waiting for spring according to the calendar. At the date when, by the calendar, winter begins, the earth is really at its nearest to the sun, and this has so mysterious an influence in our northern hemisphere, wrapped though it be in the snows of winter, that when January comes the world of plants and animals is awakened as if by a magician's wand. The buds are already forming and many of the animals are beginning to procreate their kind. I read recently in Francé's[36]) book that the most notable scientific and literary productions come into the world in the months of January and February. In the life of mankind, just as much as in that of all other beings, the winter solstice is a critical hour, one at which the current of the vital forces receives a fresh impetus. You too, Sonichka, are one of these early flowers that bloom amid snow and ice. Such flowers are apt to feel a trifle chilly, not perfectly at ease in life, so that they need tender care.

I was so delighted with the Rodin[37]) you sent me at Christmas, and should have written to thank you at once, had not Mathilde told me you were at Frankfort. What especially charms me in Rodin is his feeling for nature, his respect for every blade of grass in the field. He must have been a splendid creature, frank and natural, overflowing with warmth and intelligence; he strongly reminds me of Jaurès[38]). What did you think of my Broodcoorens?[39]) Or did you know the book already? I was much taken with his novel. The descriptions of landscape, especially, are of great imaginative force. Broodcoorens, like De Coster[40]) evidently thinks that the sun rises and sets in Flanders far more splendidly than anywhere else in the world. The Flemings are passionately in love with their country, they describe it, not so much as a beautiful part of the earth's surface, but rather as if it were to them a radiant young bride. The gloomy and tragical close of the book reminded me of the tremendous imagery of *Till Eulenspiegel*[41]). Don't you find that the "colour" of these books recalls Rembrandt?[42]) There is the same sombreness of the general picture, but mingled with the glint of old gold; there is the same startling realism in details, and yet a general impression of imaginative mystery is conveyed.

In the *Berliner Tageblatt*[43]) I read that a new Titian[44]) has been hung in the Friedrich Museum. Have you been to see it? Titian is not one of my favourites. His pictures seem to me over-elaborated, over-refined. cold. Forgive me if I am committing lese-majesty. but I always let my feelings guide me in such matters. Still I should be very glad if I could visit the Friedrich Museum to greet the new guest.

I have been reading a number of books on Shakespeare, written in the sixties and seventies when the Shakespeare problem was still being vigorously discussed in Germany. I wish you would try to get me the following books from the Royal Library or the Reichstag Library: L. Klein. *History of Italian Drama;* Schack, *History of Dramatic Literature in Spain;* Gervinus and Ulrici's books on Shakespeare. What is your own feeling about Shakespeare? Write soon. All my love.

Keep cheerful, whatever happens. Darling Sonichka, good-bye.

When are you coming to see me?

Sonyusha, will you be so good as to send Mathilde some hyacinths from me? I will pay you for them when you come.

Your Rosa

Breslau, March 24, 1918.

My dearest Sonichka,

It is such a terribly long time since I last wrote, but you have been often in my mind. One thing after another seems to take away my wish to write . . . If we could only be together, strolling through the countryside and talking of whatever might come into our heads — but there is no chance of it at present. My petition for release was rejected, to the accompaniment of a detailed description of my incorrigible wickedness; a request for a brief furlough had no better fate. I shall have to stay here, apparently, till we have conquered the whole world!

Sonyusha, when a long time passes without my having any news from you, I always get the impression that in your loneliness — uneasy, miserable and even desperate — you must be as helpless as a leaf driven before the wind. The idea makes me very unhappy. But just think, spring has come again, the days are growing so long and so light; there must already be a great deal to see and to listen to in the country. Go out as much as you can; the sky is now so interesting and so variegated with the clouds restlessly chasing one another, the chalky soil, where none of the crops have yet begun to show, must be lovely in the changing lights. Feast your eyes on it all, so that I can see it through you.

That is the only thing of which one never tires, the only thing which perpetually retains the charm of novelty and remains inviolably faithful. For my sake, too, you positively must go to the Botanical Gardens, so that you can tell me all about them. Something exceedingly strange is happening this spring. The birds have come north four to six weeks earlier than usual. The nightingale arrived here on March 10th; the wryneck, which is not due till the end of April, was heard laughing as early as March 15th; the golden oriole, which is sometimes called "the Whitsun bird", and which is never seen till May, was already uttering its flutelike note in the grey sky before dawn fully a week ago. I can hear them all from a distance when they sing in the grounds of the lunatic asylum. I can't think what the meaning of this premature migration is. I wonder sometimes whether the same thing is happening in other places, or whether the influence of the lunatic asylum is responsible for the early return to the particular spot. Do go to the Botanical Gardens, Sonichka, towards noon when the sun is shining brightly, and let me know all you can hear. Over and above the issue of the battle of Cambrai, this really seems to me the most important thing in the world.

The pictures you have sent me are lovely. Needless to say a word about the Rembrandt. As for the Titian, I was even more struck by the horse than by the rider; I should not have thought it possible to depict so much power, so much majesty, in an animal. But the most beautiful of all is

Bartolommeo Veneziano's[15]) *Portrait of a Lady.* I knew nothing of the work of this artist. What a frenzy of colour, what delicacy of line, what a mysterious charm of expression! In a vague sort of way the *Lady* reminds me of *Mona Lisa*[16]). Your pictures have brought a flood of joy and light into my prison cell.

Of course you must keep Hans Dieffenbach's book. It grieves me that all his books should not have come into *our* hands. I would rather have given them to you than to anyone. Did the Shakespeare reach you in good time? What news from Karl, and when do you expect to see him again? Give him a thousand greetings from me, and a message: "This, too, will pass." Keep your spirits up; enjoy the spring; when the next one comes, we shall all enjoy it together. Best love. Happy Easter!

Love, too, to the children.

Your Rosa

Breslau, May 2, 1918.

I have been reading *Candide*[47]) and Countess Alfeld's[48]) *Memoirs*, and have enjoyed them both immensely. *Candide* is in such a beautiful edition that I had not the heart to cut the leaves, but read it just as it was. Since it was only uncut at the top, I managed all right. This spiteful collection of all the miseries of mankind would probably before the war have seemed to me nothing but caricature, to-day, however, it has produced quite a realistic impression . . . And now at length, I know the course of a phrase I have myself used occasionally: *Mais il faut cultiver notre jardin*[49]). Countess Alfeld's book is an interesting picture of a phase of civilisation and supplements Grimmelhausen's[50]) message . . . What are you doing? Aren't you enjoying this glorious spring weather?

Always your

Rosa

✓ *Breslau, May 12. 1918.*

Sonichka,

Your little note gave me so much pleasure that I must answer it at once. You see what enjoyment you got out of your visit to the Botanical Gardens, and how enthusiastic you are about it. Why don't you go there oftener? I assure you that it means a great deal to me when you promptly record your impressions with such warmth and colour. Yes, I know those wonderful crimson flowers of the spruce-fir. They are so incredibly beautiful (as, indeed, are most other trees when in bloom) that one can hardly believe one's eyes. There are the female flowers, out of which the great cones grow, to hang point downwards when their weight increases, beside them are the far less conspicuous pale-yellow male flowers of the spruce, the ones that furnish the golden pollen. — I don't know the "pettoria". You write that it is a kind of acacia. Do you mean that it has pinnate leaves, and has blossoms like those of the sweet pea, thus resembling the pseudo-acacia? I suppose you know that the tree commonly spoken of as the acacia is really a "robinia". The true acacia is a mimosa; it has sulphur-yellow flowers with an intoxicating perfume; but I don't think it would grow in Berlin in the open, for it is a sub-tropical plant. When

5

I was in Corsica, at Ajaccio in December I saw splendid mimosas, huge trees, blooming in the great square . . . Here, unfortunately, I can only watch the crests of the trees that show over the top of the wall a long way off. I see them turning green, and try to guess their species from the tint and general shape. The other day some one brought a fallen branch into the house. Its strange aspect attracted much attention, and every one wanted to know what it could be. It was an elm! Do you remember how in my own street in the South End I showed you an elm laden with fragrant pinkish-green clusters? This was in May, too, and you were delighted with the wonderful sight. Here people live for years and decades in a street planted with elms without ever "noticing", what an elm tree looks like when it is in flower. They are just as unobservant as regards animals. Most townfolk are really barbarians.

For my part, however, my interest in organic nature is almost morbid in its intensity. A pair of crested larks here have one young bird — no doubt the other three have come to a bad end. This little one can already run. You may have noticed the quaint way in which crested larks run. They trip along with short, hasty steps, not like the sparrow which hops on both feet. This young lark can fly quite well by now, but is not yet able to find its own food (insects, grubs, etc.) at any rate while the weather is still so cold. Every evening in the court beneath my window, it utters its sharp, plaintive pipe. The old birds promptly put in an appearance, answering with a soft and anxious "hweet, hweet", and they bustle about to hunt up some food in the chill evening twilight. As soon as they find anything, it is stuffed down the throat of the clamorous youngster. This happens evening after evening at about half past eight, and when I hear the shrill note of the fledgling and watch the eager solicitude of the parent birds I have quite a pang. I can do nothing to help, for these crested larks are timid. If I throw out crumbs they only fly away, being very different from the pigeons and the sparrows, which follow me about like dogs. It is no use for me to tell myself not to be silly, seeing that I am not responsible for all the hungry little larks in the world, and that I cannot shed tears over all the thrashed buffaloes in the world (they still come here day after day drawing the lorries laden with bags). Logic does not help in the matter, and it makes me ill to see suffering. In the same way, though the chattering of the starling during the livelong day is tiresome, at times, if the bird is silent for a day or two, I get no rest from the feeling that something must have happened to it. I wait and wait for the nonsense talk to be resumed, so that I can be reassured as to my starling's safety. Thus passing out of my cell in all directions are fine threads connecting me with thousands of creatures great and small, whose doings react upon me to arouse disquiet, pain, and self-reproach. You yourself, too, belong to this company of birds and beasts to which my nature throbs responsive. I feel how you are suffering because the years are passing beyond recall without your being able really to "live"! Have patience, and take courage! We shall live none the less, shall live through great experiences. What we are now witnessing is the submergence of the old world, day by day another fragment sinks beneath the waters, day by day

5*

there is some fresh catastrophe. The strangest thing is that most people see nothing of it, but continue to imagine that the ground is firm beneath their feet.

Sonichka, do you happen to have *Gil Blas* and *The Devil on two Sticks* or can you get them for me? I have never read Le Sage's[51]) books, and have long wanted to do so. Do you know them? If you have not got them, buy them in a cheap edition.

Much love

Your Rosa

Write soon to let me know how Karl is.

Perhaps Pfemfert has a copy of *Flachsacker*[52]) by Stijn Streuvels[53]), another Fleming. It has been published by the *Inselverlag*[54]) and is said to be very good.

Breslau, October 18, 1918.

Darling Sonichka,

I wrote to you the day before yesterday. So far I have had no answer to the telegram I sent to the Imperial Chancellor; I may have to wait several days for an answer. But this much is certain, in my present mood I can no longer endure to receive my friends' visits under the supervision of the warders. I have borne it patiently all these years, and in other circumstances I should have continued to bear it. But the complete change in the general situation has had its reaction upon my own psychology. To carry on a conversation under supervision, to find it impossible to talk about the things that really interest me would now be intolerable. I would rather forego having visitors until we are all at liberty once more.

Things can't go on like this much longer. Now that Dittmann[55]) and Kurt Eisner[56]) have been set free, I am sure that the door will soon be open for myself, and for Karl too. We had better wait until we can meet in Berlin.

Till then, much love.

Always your

Rosa

NOTES

[1]) Pet name for Sophie Liebknecht, wife of Karl Liebknecht. R. L. sometimes uses the diminutive form Sonichka. Occasionally it is Sonyusha. — Karl Liebknecht, son of Wilhelm Liebknecht, was born in 1871, and was murdered, like R. L., on the night of January, 15th, 1919.

[2]) John Galsworthy's novel.

[3]) Helmi and Bobbi (mentioned in the next letter) are the Liebknecht sons.

[4]) A German poet, novelist, and translator. Born 1770, died 1843.

[5]) Captain in the French navy, born 1850, famous novelist.

[6]) A town in the former German province Posen.

[7]) Written on the day when Karl Liebknecht was sentenced to four years hard labour.

[8]) German dramatist, born 1862. The best-known of his numerous plays, "The Weavers", published in 1892, had as his theme the Silesian labour troubles of the year 1844.

[9]) German novelist, born 1875. His favourite topic is the life of the rich mercantile class of Hamburg.

[10]) German poet, born 1804, died 1875.

[11]) Austrian composer, born 1860, died 1903. Celebrated as a writer of songs.

[12]) Goethe, German poet, dramatist, and philosopher, born 1749, died 1832, rewrote this celebrated folk-tale, of which the earliest versions extant date from a thousand years back. In the form of a romance describing the doings of the fox and the other beasts, the fable contains a satire on contemporary manners, and especially on the lives of the clergy.

[13]) German poet and dramatist, born 1759, died 1805.

[14]) Russian novelist, born 1821, died 1881.

[15]) German dramatic composer, born 1813, died 1883, "The Meistersinger", an opera, depicts a competition among the mastersingers in the Middle Ages.

[16]) "West Eastern Diwan", — a long collection of poems by Goethe, published in 1819. In the form of an oriental allegory it deals, in part, with the social problems of the day.

[17]) "Flower Greeting".

[18]) A town on the Oder, capital of Silesia.

[19]) French painter, a peasant by birth. (1814—1875).

[20]) A statue of Venus, discovered in 1820 on the island of Milo in the Aegean Sea. Now in the Louvre Museum. Paris.

[21]) French composer, born 1818, died 1893.

[22]) Anacreon's Grave.

[23]) Dr. Hans Dieffenbach, one of R. L.'s most intimate friends, killed in the war.

[24]) One of the most noted of living French authors, and a member of the Communist Party. Born 1844.

[25]) The Gods are athirst.

[27]) The Lessing Legend, a book by Franz Mehring, author of "The Standard of life of Karl Marx" etc.

[27]) Richard Dehmel. German poet, born 1863, died 1921

[28]) German poet and dramatist, born 1863.

[29]) German author, born 1862.

[30]) Stephan George, contemporary German poet, described by some of his admirers as the greatest of all living poets.

[31]) German poet and playwright, born 1796, died 1835.

[32]) The Fatal Fork, a satirical comedy.

[33]) Song by Goethe.

[34]) Born in 1828, died 1875. In addition to the well-known "History of Materialism", Lange wrote a widely-read work, "The Labour Question, its Significance for the Present and the Future". Socialist in outlook, he was greatly interested in the foundation of the First International.

[35]) Woe to the conquered.

[36]) Raoul H. Francé, Austrian author and man of science. writing on Darwinism and kindred topics. Born 1874.

[37]) French sculptor and etcher, born 1840, died 1917.

[38]) French statesman and man of letters, for many years leader of the United French Socialist Party. Born 1859, assassinated July 31, 1914.

[39]) Pierre Broodcoorens, contemporary author, a Fleming, but writes in French.

[40]) Charles de Coster, another contemporary Flemish author whose chosen medium is the French tongue.

[41]) A German folk-tale, dating from early in the sixteenth century, describing the pranks and adventures of a semilegendary figure, Till Eulenspiegel by name, a handicraftsman who wandered through Germany during the first half of the fourteenth century.

[42]) Dutch painter, born 1606, died 1669.

[43]) One of the most noted of the daily newspapers of Berlin.

[44]) Painter of the Venetian school, born about 1477, died 1576.

[45]) Bartolommeo Veneziano, Italian painter, pupil of Bellini, lived in the early part of the 16th century. The "Portrait of a Lady" is dated 1530.

[46]) Famous picture by Leonardo da Vinci, an Italian painter, sculptor, engineer, and architect, born 1452, died 1519.

[47]) A satirical romance, by Voltaire, French author and philosopher, born 1694, died 1778.

[48]) Leonora Christina, Countess Alfeld, was daughter of Christian IV., King of Denmark. In connection with her husbands political intrigues she was imprisoned from 1663 to 1685 in the Blue Tower of the Royal Palace at Copenhagen. Her Memoirs ("Jammersminde", — memoirs of sorrow) have been translated intö many languages. The German version had evidently been sent to Rosa Luxemburg as appropriate reading for another prisoner of State.

[49]) In French in the original It means: We must cultivate our garden, i. e. must attend to our own affaires.

[50]) Hans Jakob Christoffel von Grimmelshausen, German author, born about 1625, died 1676, led an adventurous life during the Thirty Years War, and was a pioneer writer of the picaresque romance or novel of adventure.

[51]) French author and dramatist, born 1668, died 1747.

[52]) The Field of Flax.

[53]) Pen-name of Frank Lateur, born 1872, writes in the Flemish tongue.

[54]) A well-known publishing house in Leipzig.

[55]) German Social Democrat, born 1871. As member of the German Reichstag, he was one of those who from 1916 onwards voted against the war credits. A member of the Independent group which seceded from the Social Democratic Party. Entered into a fresh alliance with the S. D. P. after the German revolution of November 9, 1918, and helped to form the provisional government. At present member of the N. E. C. of the United Social Democratic Party of Germany.

[56]) German (Bavarian) Socialist politician and author, born 1867, frequently imprisoned for "sedition" and kindred offences. President of the revolutionary government in Bavaria. Assassinated by a reactionary nobleman on February 21, 1919.

AFTERWORD

Rosa Luxemburg was born May 5th, 1871, in a small town in Poland. In spite of the poverty of her parents there was a desire for and an appreciation of intellectual attainments. Her mother, especially, of whom Rosa always spoke and wrote with such tenderness, seems to have maintained a high standard for the family. The language of the household was not Yiddish, but Polish. The books the family read were not the *Talmud*, but the classics.

Rosa entered the Girls' High School in Warsaw at an unusually early age. She graduated at fifteen, with the highest honours and would have received the gold medal had it not been that already she was suspected of political tendencies inimical to the government of the "little father" in St. Petersburg. For three years after her graduation she devoted herself to literature, *belles lettres*, in a circle of friends more liberal than revolutionary, although sufficiently revolutionary to bring down upon themselves the attention of the vigilant police of the Czar. At the age of eighteen Rosa was compelled to leave Russian-Poland and flee to Zurich, that famous city-of-refuge of European political refugees. In Zurich she studied in the University, especially Mathematics and Natural Science.

Among her fellow students were a number of Polish and Russian exiles and their friends, and the family with whom she lived, brought her within the ranks of the revolutionists. It must have been a test of the spirit of the young woman. On the one hand, among her young friends, she had the zest of youth and its dreams of a nobler, finer, free world. On the other, in the house where she lived, she witnessed the effects of the struggle upon the souls, who had devoted themselves to the pursuit of this ideal. The Lubeck family were also exiles, from Germany, where the father had been a member of the Social Democratic party. He lay, now, helpless and ill, confined to his bed, unable even to write. His wife, the mother of a large family of children, had grown weary of the battle, longed only to free herself from the sordid weary round of her daily life, and was discontented, unhappy, impatient.

As if they had been her own people Rosa undertook to hold this group together. She wrote at the dictation of the father, helped the mother over her mental and spiritual struggles, gathered the children about her, and succeeded in bringing peace and serenity and new hope and spirit into the family. It was an excellent training for the work she was to do in future, in a larger field. But even now she was approaching Socialism, not from the angle of bound spirits seeking freedom, but from the scientific basis laid down, by Marx and Engels whom she read and studied during this period.

In the years between 1889 and 1892 she studied, now in Zurich, now in Berne, and again in Genoa, Socialism and History. During these years she met Plechanov and Axelrod, and drew about her and them a circle of Polish revolutionists, Karski, Leo Jogisches, and others, and sought to introduce the science of Marx into the political life of these youths. Up to this time the Polish rebels hat found expression in terrorism alone, holding their organisation together by conspirative measures and plans. Their chief leader was Dazynski, wo believed that a social revolution was possible for Poland only after it had become independent of Russia.

Up to this time there had been but one day in the year that might be called a day of freedom for the workers of Russia. It was the 1st of May, a day when workers might leave their places of employment and attend meetings or demonstrations or hold parades. Doubtless it was granted by the Czar's government all the more cheerfully because it indicated to the police the strength and fervour of the masses and brought forward new leaders and new objects for persecution. It was, however, greeted by the workers with special literary productions, and among these, on May 1st, 1892, was a brochure written by Rosa Luxemburg. It was not printed, however, because it was written. not in prose, but in hexameters.

This was the beginning of Rosa Luxemburg's real struggle. Up to this time she had only been in training.

In 1893 she was barred from the International Congress held in Zurich, on the charge that her organisation — the Polish Revolutionary Party — was one of spies and informers. Undaunted by this terrible blow she persisted in her efforts to base the Polish revolution on scientific Marxism, proclaiming ever her sincere conviction that Poland's hope and salvation lay only in a union of the working class of Poland with the working class of Russia and their combined struggle against the bourgeoisie.

In 1895 she went to Paris, studied Polish History in the National Library, and wrote two famous articles, published serially: *The Industrial Development of Poland*, and *Social Patriotism in Poland.* In 1896 she attended the International Congress in London. This was a victory that must have healed whatever wound remained after her Zurich experience three years before. In the autumn of that year, in order to obtain a standing in the German Social Democratic Party she entered college and by the 1st of May, 1897, she had attained the degree of L. L. D. The *magna cum laude* was not to be hers, although she had won it and it was recommended by her professors, because the faculty council decided "that is, for a woman, too much".

There remained another condition still unfulfilled. In order to live in Germany and work in the Social Democratic Party without being subject to banishment, she must become a German citizen. This was arranged by a formal, nominal, marriage to a son of the Lubeck family in Zurich, and, pausing only long enough to make the necessary arrangements for an immediate divorce, she left for Germany on the day of her marriage.

In the years immediately following, in agitation among the masses, in party activities, and especially in the crisis that followed upon the publication of Edward Bernstein's *Problems of Socialism*, she played on a larger stage the same role she had played in her student days in Zurich, supporting the weak and uncertain as she had held together the Lubeck family. A series of her articles, *Social Reform or Revolution* in the Leipzig *Volkszeitung* — a paper which she afterwards edited for a short time — not only cleared up the doubts and questions raised by Bernstein, but made her a factor to be reckoned with. In 1905, the year of the Russian revolution, she crystallised revolutionary thought in another series of articles — *The Aim and Goal of the Proletariat in Revolution.* Her solution to this was "the Dictatorship of the Proletariat".

In this same year she made a journey to Warsaw under an assumed name, was arrested and spent more than three months in prison. In the succeeding years she grew ever more and more impatient of opportunists, compromisers, and users of empty phrases. She was the brains and leader of the party school. She made enemies among the members of the party, by her uncompromising stand. There was even a motion to expel her from the ranks of the party.

Already, in 1910, the first clouds of the imperialist war were appearing on the horizon. The immediate threat of war began to submerge the minds of the masses; its problems to supersede those of theories and party tactics. Now all her energies were thrown into the struggle against militarism. She did not lose her grasp of Marxian science, even here. Her book on *The Accumulation of Capital* was written while she was travelling over Germany, speaking from platforms, proclaiming — "When we are ordered to shoot our French brothers we shall say, **No**, that we will **not do**".

One visions from a recital of the facts of her

history a strong, a courageous, a fervent, but an eager impatient soul. The vision is true, but incomplete. She was also sensitive, tender, and — as these letters show — immeasurably gentle and considerate. Her iteration of the words "Be cheerful and serene" addressed to a friend who — despite grievous anxieties — was still enjoying that freedom from which Rosa herself was debarred; her rare plaints at the circumstances of her own fate, no less than the intimate revelations of her apprehension of beauty in all things; her keen and sensitive response to the smallest manifestations of Nature — all these combine to place this well rounded and well nigh complete nature and soul so high that one must bow reverently before it. Her cool, clear, scientific brain; the ardour of her courageous and daring spirit; and this almost ecstatic beauty-loving soul — what an ideal and what a model!

Not only because she was, in theory, in heart and soul, and in activity, an internationalist, but because she was a great spirit and a great soul, does Rosa Luxemburg belong to *all* the world. The Poland of her birth, the Germany of her later labours, hold her no more than Italy holds the spirit of Leonardo da Vinci or Greece holds Socrates. The soul that sets out upon the great search for truth, for beauty, and for freedom traverses the whole world — perchance the whole Universe — and belongs to *all*, even as it embraces *all*.

Not because she fell, a martyr in the struggle, but because she lived and fought and suffered and kept her courage and her spirit, does Rosa Luxemburg take her place among the heroes and heroines of life. Not only because she saw clearly and pointed the way, but because she visioned beauty and love along the way, does her figure stand as a guide post and an inspiration. The struggles of the working class are and must be bitter always, dark sometimes, hopeless appearing often, but now and then a gleam from the torch that Rosa Luxemburg carried so high must light the path for a moment, must bring new hope and new strength.

Zeitfracht Medien GmbH
Ferdinand-Jühlke-Straße 7
99095 Erfurt, Deutschland
produktsicherheit@kolibri360.de